Simple Science Experiments

by Andrea McLoughlin
Illustrated by Lynn Adams

Cartwheel
B·O·O·K·S ®

SCHOLASTIC INC.
New York Toronto London Auckland Sydney

For the scientist in all of us
—A.M.

To my son Isaac and our cat Maxine
—L.A.

ISBN 0-590-48589-X

Text copyright © 1996 by Andrea McLoughlin.
Illustrations copyright © 1996 by Lynn Adams.
All rights reserved. Published by Scholastic Inc.
CARTWHEEL BOOKS and the CARTWHEEL BOOKS logo
are registered trademarks of Scholastic Inc.

12 11 10 9 8 7 6 5 4 3 2 1   6 7 8 9/9 0 1/0

Printed in the U.S.A.   24

First Scholastic printing, February 1996

Contents

LIQUIDS

KITCHEN SCIENCE

You have a little bit of scientist in you!

It's the part of you that likes to explore and try new things, to look at the world around you, and to think about how things work.

Are you ready to be a scientist?
Grab a pencil.

Use a separate notebook to keep a science journal.
Record your findings in words or pictures as you work through this book.

Be careful!
Some of these experiments and activities need a grown-up's help.
Ask a grown-up to work with you—then he or she can have fun with science, too!

LIQUIDS

Count the Drops

How many drops of water can you
fit on top of a penny?

Lay a penny flat on a table.
Guess how many drops will fit on it.
Write the number in your journal.

Hold an eyedropper full of water
just a little above the penny.
Gently squeeze out one drop at a time.
Count the drops.

How many drops does the penny
hold before the water spills?
Compare this number with the number you guessed.
Did the penny take more or fewer drops than you
thought it would?

Add More Drops

What happens as you add drops on top of the penny?

Water drops stick to other water drops. Water has a thin "skin" that helps to keep the drops together until there's too much water for the skin to hold. This skin is the water's *surface tension*.

How many drops will stay on top of a nickel? On a quarter? Write your prediction—what you think will happen— in your journal. Then record your actual results.

Chase the Pepper

Shake some pepper on top of a bowl of water.
The water's surface tension holds the floating
pepper in place.

Wet your finger and rub it on a bar of soap.
Touch your finger to the water in the bowl.

The soap weakens the water's surface tension where you touch the water.

The pepper gets pulled to where the water's surface tension is stronger—around the edge of the bowl.

What else can you float on water before you break the water's surface tension?
Rinse the bowl well before every try!

Make Mysterious Milk Streamers

Measure ½ cup of milk.
Pour it into a clean bowl.
Add some drops of food coloring.
Use different colors and don't stir!
Now add a few drops of liquid dishwashing soap.

What is happening in the bowl?
Write what you see—your observation—in your notebook.

The soap breaks the surface tension of the milk. It also breaks apart tiny drops of milk fat, which you can't see.
The colors get pushed and pulled around as this happens.

After the colors have stopped moving, can you find a way to get them moving again?

KITCHEN SCIENCE

Create Your Own Milk Glue

Many things can be made from milk:
butter, cheese, ice cream—even glue!

Measure ½ cup of milk into a small cooking pot.
Ask a grown-up to heat the milk slowly, stirring it until it's
hot, but not boiling, and then remove the pot from the
heat.

Add 2 teaspoons of vinegar.
Stir this mixture.
Lumps will form.

Have a grown-up pour off the liquid and rinse the lumps in cold water.
The lumps are a milk protein called *casein*.
Now, put the lumps in a small mixing bowl and add ¼ teaspoon of baking soda.

Slowly add a little water and stir until the mixture becomes pasty.

You've made milk glue!
Try using it to paste papers or art projects together.

Have a Ketchup Race

Many people like their ketchup to be thick.

Choose three different kinds of ketchups.
Label the first one, 1, the second, 2, and the third, 3.
Take a piece of cardboard and lay it on your table.
Draw three circles in a row at the top of the cardboard.
Write 1, 2, and 3 in the circles.

Bend the last three inches of the cardboard up to keep the ketchup from spilling off the bottom.

Pile some thick books together on the table.
Put 2 tablespoons of ketchup 1 into circle 1.
Put the same amount of ketchup 2 in circle 2, and
ketchup 3 in circle 3.

Make a prediction.
Which one do you think will win? Why?
To start the race, quickly stand up the cardboard and
lean it against the books.
Remember, the slowest ketchup wins!

Take a ketchup survey.
Ask your friends and family to taste the ketchups.
Which ketchup is the winner now?

Eye Those Bones

Save some chicken bones from a meal
(small bones work well).
Clean and dry them.

Look at the bones. Feel them.
Try to bend them.
Write your observations in your journal.

Put one bone in a cup of your favorite soda.
Put another bone in water.
Put a third bone in vinegar.
Leave one bone dry.
Every four days, replace the liquids in the cups
with more of the same liquids.
Check the bones and write down
any changes in how they look, feel, and bend.

Remember your teeth are bones, too.
Try this with baby teeth that have fallen out.

WEATHER

Make Your Own Sun Clock

Find a large, sunny area near you.
Stand a long stick in a lump of clay in the
middle of the sunny spot.

Go to this spot every hour and put a rock on the
ground at the end of the stick's shadow.
Write the time on the rocks with chalk or paint.

What shape is your sun clock?
How can you check if it is telling the right time?
Does it work in winter, spring, summer, and fall?

9

10

11

17

Have an Ice Cube Contest

Can you find the best place to melt an ice cube?
Challenge your friends to an ice cube meltdown!

Make ice cubes that are the same size.
To do this, measure the water that you
put in each cup of an ice tray.
Freeze the tray for one day.

Then go outside with your friends.
Have everyone choose a spot that he or she
thinks will be best for melting an ice cube.
Quickly give out the ice cubes.
Place them in the chosen spots.

Whose ice cube melts the fastest?
Why do you think that spot is the
best for melting the ice cube?

19

Catch Raindrops

Dress yourself in rain gear and spend a minute in a light rain holding a bowl of flour.

Warning! Do not do this in a thunderstorm!

Watch what happens as raindrops hit the flour.
(You can make raindrops by watering a leafy branch and shaking it over a bowl of flour.)
Go inside and carefully spoon the raindrops into a strainer.
Shake the strainer gently
to remove loose flour.

The beads you have left
are floured raindrops!

Record your findings in your journal.
Are all of the raindrops the same shape?
Are they all the same size?
How can you measure them?
Draw pictures of the raindrops.

Go out again in another rain shower.
Do the same experiment.
How are the raindrops the same?
How are they different?

PLANTS

Discover a Baby Plant

You can find a baby plant inside a seed.
Soak several large lima beans in water for a
few hours.
When they're soft, peel off the thin outer covering.

What do you think this "seed coat" does?

Right! It protects the seed.

Carefully pull apart the two halves of the bean.
Look inside.
Can you find the baby plant?

The baby plant in the seed is very tiny.
The large bean that you split open is food for the baby plant to use until it can grow leaves and make its own food.

Start Those Seeds

Do seeds need water to grow?

Fold a napkin and place it around the inside of a see-through cup.
Tuck some lima beans between the paper towel and the cup.
Set up another cup the same way, but add some water to this one.

Put the dry cup and the wet cup next to each other and watch them for a few days.
Add water to the wet cup if the paper towel starts to dry.

What happens to the seeds in the cups?
What does this tell you?
Try sprouting different kinds of seeds!

Grow an Upside-down Plant

Can plants tell up from down?

Open the top of a clean, empty milk carton.
Ask a grown-up to poke three holes near the
top of the carton.
Tie strings through them so you can hang up
the carton later.

Now, ask a grown-up to poke a small hole
in the bottom of the carton.
Carefully get a lima bean plant from the
last experiment.
Gently put the plant through the hole so that
its stem sticks out of the bottom, but its roots
are inside the milk carton.
Use a cotton ball to block up the rest of the
hole so your plant doesn't fall out.

Put some soil in the carton.
Water the soil a bit, and find a sunny place to
hang the upside-down planter.
Give your plant a little more water whenever
the soil feels too dry.

Predict what will happen to your upside-down plant
over the next few weeks.
Draw some pictures of your predictions.
Each week draw a picture of what actually
happens to your plant.
Did the plant do what you thought it would do?

ANIMALS

Take a Birdseed Survey

What kinds of seeds do the birds near you like the best?
You can investigate and find out.

You'll need an egg carton and some birdseed mix. Take the top off the egg carton and use it for an art or science project.

Separate the different seeds in the birdseed by sorting each type of seed into a different egg cup.

When you have filled the cups about halfway, place the carton outside for the birds to find.

Check the carton at least once a day, but try not to disturb the birds.

Which kind of seed do the birds like best?
How do you know?

Be a Bird-watcher!

Scientists learn about birds by watching how birds act and studying what birds do. You can, too.

What kinds of birds live near you?

Find a good bird-watching place, where you can see birds without them seeing you.

Borrow some books about birds from the library. Match the birds you see to the pictures in the books.

Then, choose one bird to watch and mark its behaviors in your journal.
You can make a chart for this information.

Does the bird hop on the ground, walk, or run?
What kind of food does it eat?
Does it sing?
What do its birdcalls sound like?
Does the bird travel alone or with others?
Does the bird bob its head or tail up and down, or flap its wings while it stands?
What else do you notice about this bird?
You can add this information to your chart, too.

Draw pictures of your bird or photograph it.
Learn the bird's name.

You can use a chart similar to the one above to study other animals, too.

CHICKADEE	
HOPS	✓
WALKS	
RUNS	
FOOD	SUET SEEDS
SONG	✓
SOUNDS LIKE:	
TRAVELS ALONE	
IN FLOCK	✓
BOBS HEAD	
BOBS TAIL	
FLAPS WINGS WHILE STANDING	✓

Catch a Chameleon

Wait! Don't cut out this chameleon!
Put a piece of paper on top of it and trace it.
Then cut out the one you traced.
Make some more paper chameleons, and you'll be
ready to play a game of chameleon camouflage!

Color the chameleons to match items around
your house—the walls, the couch, the carpet,
or the kitchen counter.
You can color the chameleons to match just
about anything!
Place them on the objects of the same color
to camouflage—or hide—them.

How long does it take for family or friends
to find them?